A Quick Guide to 18 Organizational Development Tools for Leaders

Keith B. Grant, PhD
and Melvin Rusher, PhD

Copyright © 2024 Keith B. Grant, PhD and Melvin Rusher, PhD

All rights reserved. No part of this book may be reproduced or transmitted in any form or by any means, electronic or mechanical, including photocopying, recording or by any information storage and retrieval system without permission in writing from the publisher.

Keith B. Grant Press—Novi, MI
ISBN: 979-8-218-51917-9
Library of Congress Control Number: 2024920989
Title: *A Quick Guide to 18 Organizational Development Tools for Leaders*
Author: Keith B. Grant, PhD and Melvin Rusher, PhD
Digital distribution | 2024
Paperback | 2024

Published in the United States by New Book Authors Publishing

Dedication

For *Patricia A. Grant and*

My sister, *Sharon Y. Fai*

Preface

Like it or not most of us go to work every day whether our office is at home or onsite at the organization. Problems are a fact of life for most people in modern societies. This book provides the reader with 18 useful problem-solving (PS) tools that can be used in any organization. It is easy to understand and use. The problems tool is arranged into four sections:

- What is it?
- Why use it?
- When to use it?
- Helpful Hints

Problem-Solving (PS) capabilities specific to large scale initiatives include:

- Change implementation (CI) — *Leading Change*
- Leadership effectiveness (LE) — strategic visioning; leadership alignment and roles
- Organization design (OD) — roles, governance, and structure
- Project team (PT) — structure, team development, and team dynamics
- People processes (PP) — skills, training, selection criteria, management systems, and rewards
- Culture & Systems (CS) — organizational readiness & cultural vision

The key Problem-Solving tools reinforce the PS capabilities

PS Tools	PS Capabilities					
	CI	LE	OD	PT	PP	CS
• 7-S Model	X	X	X	X	X	X
• Beckhard Model	X	X				
• Bulls-Eye Chart						
• COG's Ladder		X		X	X	X
• Denison Culture Audit		X		X		X
• Elevator Speech						
• GDQ (Group Development Questionnaire)				X		X
• *Leading Change*	X	X	X	X	X	X
• MBTI		X		X		X
• New Leader/Manager Transition		X		X		
• RASIC						
• Situational Leadership		X		X		
• Stakeholder Analysis						
• Stakeholder Workshop	X	X		X	X	
• Strategic Visioning (Grove)		X		X		
• Task Oriented Team Development (TOTD) Model		X		X		X
• Vroom Decision Making Model		X				
• William Bridges Change and Transition	X	X	X		X	X

The key Problem-Solving (PS) tools reinforce the PS capabilities

PS Tools	Page Number	
	Tool Summary	Worksheet
• 7-S Model	2	33
• Beckhard Model	4	34
• Bulls-Eye Chart	5	35
• COG's Ladder	7	36
• Denison Culture Audit	8	37
• Elevator Speech	9	38
• GDQ (Group Development Questionnaire)	11	39
• *Leading Change*	12	—
• MBTI	13	40
• New Leader/Manager Transition	14	41
• RASIC	16	42
• Situational Leadership	18	43
• Stakeholder Analysis	20	44
• Stakeholder Workshop	22	—
• Strategic Visioning (Grove)	24	45
• Task Oriented Team Development (TOTD) Model	26	46
• Vroom Decision Making Model	28	47
• William Bridges Change and Transition	30	48

Key Problem -Solving (PS) Tools

PS Tool Summary — 7-S Model

What is it?
 • A tool to introduce the organizational elements impacted by a large scale change
 • A useful framework for reviewing the impact of change across the organization
     - Highlights how changes in one part of an organization affect the rest of the organization
     - Provides direction about areas to address when implementing a change
     - Helps to evaluate the feasibility of change processes

Why use it?
 • Large scale change typically impacts all seven elements of an organization
     • Organizations which are successful at responding to change address each element
 • To highlight the importance of linking a strategy to a variety of implementation activities across the organization
 • To better understand how a change in one element impacts the other elements
     – If one of the seven elements changes, it will affect all the others
 • To highlight gaps or weaknesses in a change strategy by providing a full system view

When to use it?   • During the planning stages of a large scale change   • When leaders/project teams need to think through the impact of a change across the organization

PS Tool Illustration

Seven Elements of an Organization

- Structure
- Strategy
- Systems
- Shared Values
- Skills
- Style
- Staff

(All seven elements are interconnected in a networked diagram with Shared Values at the center.)

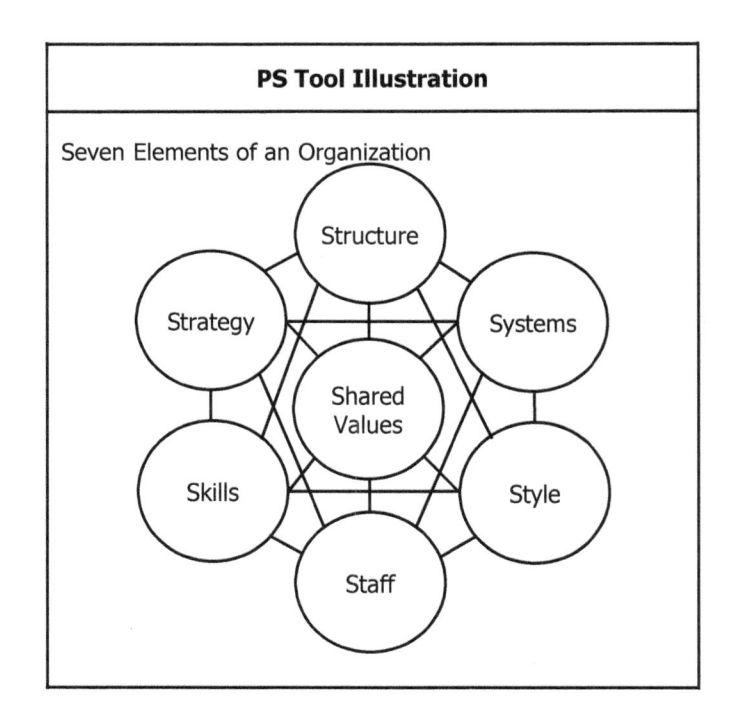

PS Tool Summary — 7-S Model (cont'd)

How to use it?
1. Clearly define the change process/strategy
2. Communicate the **shared values** and the need for change - Identify and reinforce organizational values and beliefs driving the change - Obtain input and agreement on the change vision
3. Develop the **strategy** to implement the change vision - Define the action plan required to attain this vision
4. Modify the **systems** to support the change as needed - Address systems such as IS&S, rewards, compensation, etc.
5. Ensure **staff** is informed and supportive of the change vision - Identify who will be involved/impacted by the change - Develop policies/standards regarding recruitment, appraisal, training and development, and motivation
6. Define the management **style** - Define the management approach required to support the change (i.e., self-management versus task management)
7. Ensure the **structure** is consistent with the change vision - Modify how people and resources are organized to meet the change goals
8. Define the **skills** required among employees to support the change - Establish an appropriate learning environment to support the attainment of these skills

Helpful Hints
1. The change vision needs to be clearly articulated and understood from the beginning
2. While project teams will tend to naturally address the strategy and structure elements, they need to be reminded to address the "softer" elements such as shared values, skills, staff, style, and systems - These "softer" elements are just as important as strategy and structure - Japanese companies(1) are quite effective at addressing these "softer" elements

Note: (1) 7-S was derived from studies of Japanese management techniques

PS Tool Summary — Beckhard Model

What is it?
- Process to help think through the steps necessary to get from the present state to the desired state

Why use it?
- To simplify the steps required to move through a complex change
- To help project teams recognize/address the many aspects of a change
  - Typically, we do a good job of addressing the technical aspects, but don't do as well addressing the social or political aspects of a change
  - The social and political aspects are those that typically ambush a change initiative

When to use it?
- During the initial planning stages of a change process
- As one of a few tools leveraged during a planning workshop

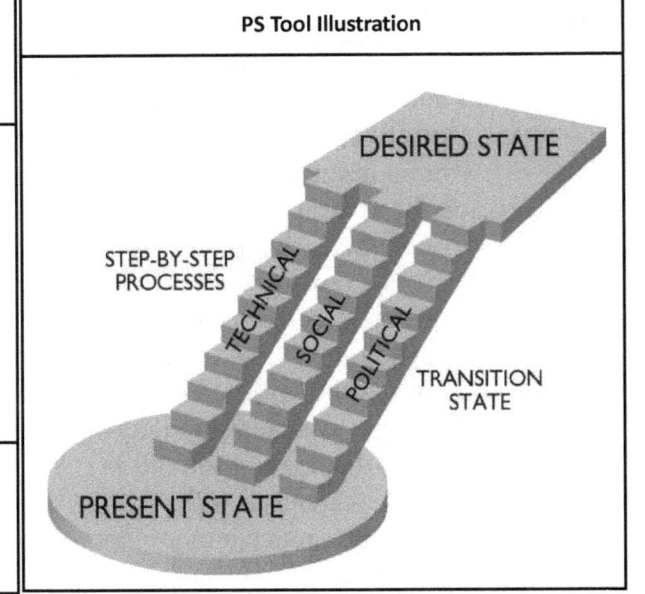

PS Tool Illustration

(Illustration: staircase diagram showing PRESENT STATE at bottom leading via STEP-BY-STEP PROCESSES labeled TECHNICAL, SOCIAL, POLITICAL — the TRANSITION STATE — up to DESIRED STATE at top.)

How to use it?
Led by the change project team:
1. Clearly define the desired state (vision)
• Senior managers who are championing the change need to agree on the future vision
2. Identify key aspects of the present state
3. Identify the group who will champion the change (for large scale changes only)
• A senior business leader should oversee the transition group, with input from a PS resource
4. Plan how to get from current state to desired state
• Identify the steps required (from a technical, social, and political aspect) to get to the desired state
5. Implement/reinforce plan
• Continually reassess whether you are still in the transition stages
• Determine whether you've achieved your vision

Helpful Hints
1. While this is a good model to consider for any change, it is most useful during large scale organizational change
2. Place equal emphasis on the technical, social, and political aspects of a change
• Often, the social and political aspects are overlooked or not stressed when compared to the technical aspects of a change
3. The clearer view an organization has of both its present and desired states, the easier the transition state will be

PS Tool Summary — Bulls-Eye Chart

What is it?
- The Bulls-Eye Chart helps teams begin to translate a vision of success into actionable terms

Why use it?
- The Bulls-Eye Chart helps teams to:
    1. Identify behaviors that both support and detract from the team's vision of successful implementation of the solution(s) to the issue(s) they are resolving
    2. Begin to identify what underlies the behaviors that detract from success — the "less of" — to help think through appropriate engagement approaches.
    3. Start determining the supportive behaviors that may be leveraged to help the team in developing engagement approaches to facilitate the team's success
    4. Communicate with each other about team members' functions and the reason some activities and behavior occurs; this tool can make it easier for difficult issues to be "put on the table"

When to use it?
- Bulls-Eye Chart is best applied early in the *Leading Change* cycle, typically for the Defining What To Do lever

PS Tool Illustration

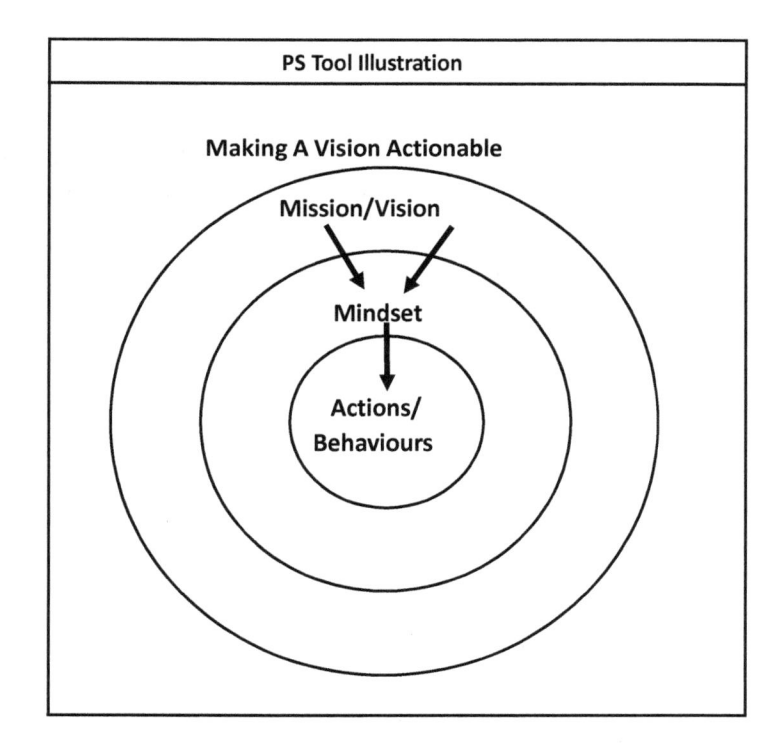

Making A Vision Actionable

Mission/Vision → Mindset → Actions/Behaviours

PS Tool Summary — Bulls-Eye Chart (cont'd)

How to use it?
1. As a group, review the team's vision of success (e.g., output from the Backward Imaging or Visioning Questions)
2. Determine the required changes in attitudes/perceptions necessary to support the change. It can be useful for each member to note one behavior on a Post-It and then place them on separate More of and Less of flipchart sheets
3. Review the Desired Actions/Behavioral Changes (i.e., more of and less of) lists and group similar items. When the reason a desired action or behavioral change was classified as more of or less is not clear, ask its author to explain his/her rationale
4. Ask for a volunteer to summarize the grouped Desired Actions/Behavioral Change (i.e., more of, less of) after the session for subsequent distribution to team members
5. Identify specific actions/behaviors that will create/reinforce the mindset and achieve the vision. This should take the form of ideas that should be built in to the Action Plan. This can typically be good input for building Action Plan steps needed for increasing the engagement needed for successful implementation
6. Summarize these step 5 implications and distribute to the team for reference in building the Action Plan

Helpful Hints
1. Encourage the team leader(s) to have team members individually identify Desired Actions/ Behavioral Changes to prevent dominant team members from overriding less dominant team members
2. Determine the most effective means of brainstorming that will elicit all team members' views of relevant Desired Actions/Behavioral Changes with the team leader(s)
3. In grouping similar actions and behavioral changes, be cautious not to lose any of the noted items unless team members unanimously opt to discard the behavior (i.e., the author changes his/her view)
4. Leave sufficient time to discuss step 5 above (i.e., implications for the Action Plan); This can serve as a key input to identifying steps needed to build engagement for the Action Plan

PS Tool Summary — Cog's Ladder

What is it?
• A model to understand the different stages of group development   – Every group undergoes discrete stages starting at the polite stage when the group is first established

Why use it?
• To assist a group in transitioning through the different stages of group development and in accomplishing its goals • To help a group to understand that they will go through different phases and how to deal with each of these phases   – The group will better understand some of the uncomfortable feelings they'll experience as they transition through the stages of group development • To help a group to identify the phase they are in as they aspire to achieve an Esprit d'core • Because a group will go back down the ladder when a new team member is added

When to use it?
• When team conflicts/issues arise • When the team appears to be stuck in the 'Bid for Power' stage and not accomplishing its goals

PS Tool Illustration

Stages of Group Development (bottom to top):
- Polite
- Why We're Here
- Bid for Power
- Constructive
- Esprit

How to use it?
1. PS Resource would identify a team stuck in one of the stages and recommend the use of Cog's ladder
2. Plan a workshop, to be facilitated by a PS resource to review the Cog's Ladder theory
• Introduce the team to the different stages of group development
• Facilitate a group discussion to identify what stage the team is currently in
• Identify key behaviors that need to change to transition to the next stage
• Define next steps for the group
3. Follow-up with the group to ensure that they have progressed beyond the current stage
• Review key principles of Cog's Ladder
• Celebrate group advancement

Helpful Hints
1. Similar to riding a bicycle, the first time a group climbs Cog's ladder is the hardest
• Groups seldom stay on any of the rungs for very long — they're constantly moving up and down the ladder
2. The PS resource should implement this tool on an as-needed basis to avoid overloading teams with PS tools
3. All teams go through this developmental process when they are initially formed, assigned new responsibilities, or have new team members

PS Tool Summary — Denison Culture Audit

What is it?
- A questionnaire administered to employees that assesses four cultural traits significantly impacting organizational performance:
  - Involvement
  - Consistency
  - Adaptability
  - Mission
- A process that links organizational culture and leadership practices to bottom line performance

Why use it?
- To help leaders understand how four key cultural aspects impact business deliverables
  - Helps identify organizational culture strengths and weaknesses impacting financial performance
- To ensure leaders understand where to modify/redefine the organizational culture to improve organizational effectiveness

When to use it?
- When a large scale change is introduced
  - The cultural impact of large scale change must be considered given its impact on organizational performance
- When business indicators are not moving in the desired direction, and the root cause does not appear to be linked to traditional business aspects (such as revenue, costs)

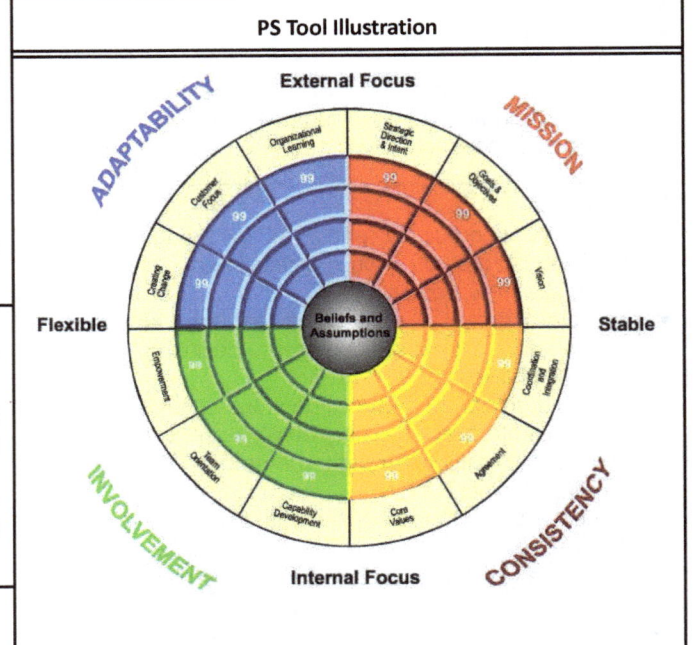

How to use it?
1. Review the Denison Culture Audit and add open ended questions as appropriate
   - Open-ended questions will help to identify more organizational-specific information
2. Administer the audit (questionnaire) to employees
3. Compile and summarize the audit results
4. Clearly communicate audit results to leadership team
   - Review interpretation guidelines
5. Identify key cultural issues that need to be addressed
6. Communicate audit results and follow-up required to organizational employees
7. Design action plans to address these cultural issues
   - Involve organizational employees as appropriate

Helpful Hints
1. Use meetings to identify additional cultural issues and to help roll-out results across organization
2. Leverage a PS 'expert' to modify/administer/interpret the Denison Culture Audit
3. Review and communicate audit results to employees in a timely manner

PS Tool Summary — Elevator Speech

What is it?
- The Elevator Speech tool is a means for the team to agree on a brief description of the initiative and agree on a consistent message to be delivered to those interested in the focus of team's initiative

Why use it?
- The two main reasons for using the Elevator Speech are that it:
    1. Helps team members understand the initiative by having them describe it in their own words. By sharing team members' individual elevator speeches, the team typically increases the understanding of the initiative and its potential impact on the company/unit
    2. Provides team members with a consistent message for all interested parties. By avoiding multiple descriptions of the team's focus, team members may better serve the initiative. This also helps in developing communiqués about the team's initiative

When to use it?
- The Elevator Speech tool is best used early in the *Leading Change* cycle, typically for the Defining What To Do lever
- This tool is best applied after the project team has defined the scope of the change needs

---

PS Tool Illustration

Designing an Elevator Speech:

1. Imagine a chance meeting with a key stakeholder in an elevator
2. The key stakeholder asks, "I heard you are working on the _____ initiative. What's it all about?"
3. Prepare and practice a short answer to that question that can be delivered in 30 seconds or less
4. Consider the following guidelines for your Elevator Speech:
    - Here's what our initiative is about
    - Here's why it is important
    - Here's what we need to change
    - Here's what success will look like
    - Here's what we need from you

PS Tool Summary — Elevator Speech (cont'd)

How to use it?
1. Team leader(s) should discuss the utility of the tool

2. Ask each team member to either individually or in pairs/groups to develop a brief Elevator Speech (that can be recited in ≤30 seconds) that describes:
   a. The initiative
   b. Why the initiative is important
   c. What needs to be changed/improved
   d. What success will look like
   e. What we need from each key stakeholder

3. Have each member or pairing/grouping of members read their Elevator Speech out loud; designate a timer
4. Capture the key messages in each of the five categories (done by the facilitator or the team leader(s)) to help in developing the Team's elevator speech
5. Based on the team members' Elevator Speeches, the leader(s) subsequently develops an overall Elevator Speech that is shared with the team

Helpful Hints
1. Before developing an Elevator Speech, team members should have been through a scoping exercise; and they should also be explained the relevance/utility of an Elevator Speech
2. Consider assigning different stakeholders to individual or groups of team members so that the "what we need from you" addresses the key stakeholders
3. There may be an advantage to assigning the Elevator Speech as "homework" to be completed between team meetings. If the team has already developed its ground rules, this can be an early litmus test of how the team members will carry out assigned accountabilities. Although this may lower the probability of task completion it may be better to have that occur early than later when lack of completion may have more negative impact on the team
4. Although crafting a good message is important and serious, the team can have some fun in reaching its Elevator Speech. Different team members can be assigned different roles: specific stakeholder; timer/elevator operator; critic; etc.
5. In the end, a consolidated team Elevator Speech should be developed based on the input from the team members. This can either be done or assigned by the team leader(s)

PS Tool Summary — Group Development Questionnaire (GDQ)

What is it?
- A statistically valid and reliable tool which measures the productivity and effectiveness of any group working together for a common purpose
- A tool that measures group (as opposed to individual) functioning
  - 60-item questionnaire with four scales
  - Measurement of group effectiveness, productivity, and development

Why use it?
- To identify team strengths and weaknesses
- To gain input that will help develop strategies to improve team effectiveness and productivity
- To help groups create a productive environment and achieve shared goals
- To benchmark a group's current status and identifies areas for growth and improvement

When to use it?
- Prior to a strategic planning process
- When there are indications that the group is not working together effectively/accomplishing its goals
- Any time a group wants to increase its overall effectiveness

PS Tool Illustration
- A diagnostic instrument with four scales:

Scale	Sample Questions
GDQ I	- Members tend to go along with whatever the leader suggests - There is very little conflict expressed in the group - We haven't discussed our goals very much
GDQ II	- People seem to have very different views about how things should be done in this group - Members challenge the leader's ideas - There is quite a bit of tension in the group at this time
GDQ III	- The group is spending its time planning how it will get its work done - We can rely on each other. We work as a team - The group is able to form subgroups, or subcommittees, to work on specific tasks
GDQ IV	- The group gets, gives, and uses feedback about its effectiveness and productivity - The group acts on its decisions - This group encourages high performance and quality work

How to use it?
1. Diagnose the productivity and effectiveness of the group
   - A certified GDQ consultant administers the GDQ questionnaire to each individual
2. Compile and summarize results of the questionnaire
   - Performed by the certified GDQ consultant
3. Present findings to the group and discuss how to address some of the key findings
   - Certified GDQ consultant leads a planning session to determine how to further develop the group
4. Follow-up on group development
   - Track progress against action plan developed
   - Continue to discuss strengths and weaknesses as a group

Helpful Hints
1. Tie the results of the GDQ to a strategic planning process
2. Leverage a certified GDQ consultant to both administer the questionnaire and facilitate action planning workshops
3. Ensure that employees are relaxed and have ample time when completing the questionnaire
   - Arrange for approximately 30 minutes of uninterrupted time to complete questionnaire

PS Tool Summary — *Leading Change*

What is it?
- *Leading Change* is an approach to large scale change implementation in which the need for engagement/buy-in is critical to success
- *Leading Change* educates change leaders and project teams on the critical success factors for implementing sustainable change
- *Leading Change* is supported by coaches who use a toolkit to help project teams integrate engagement strategies into their technical implementation plans

Why use it?
- *Leading Change* provides people with:
  - A common language to discuss change implementation
  - Practical tools and coaching support
  - A tested approach to enabling implementation teams to improve implementation effectiveness
  - Change leadership and change implementation capability

When to use it?
- For complex, large scale initiatives
- When engagement/buy-in is critical to the success of a change initiative

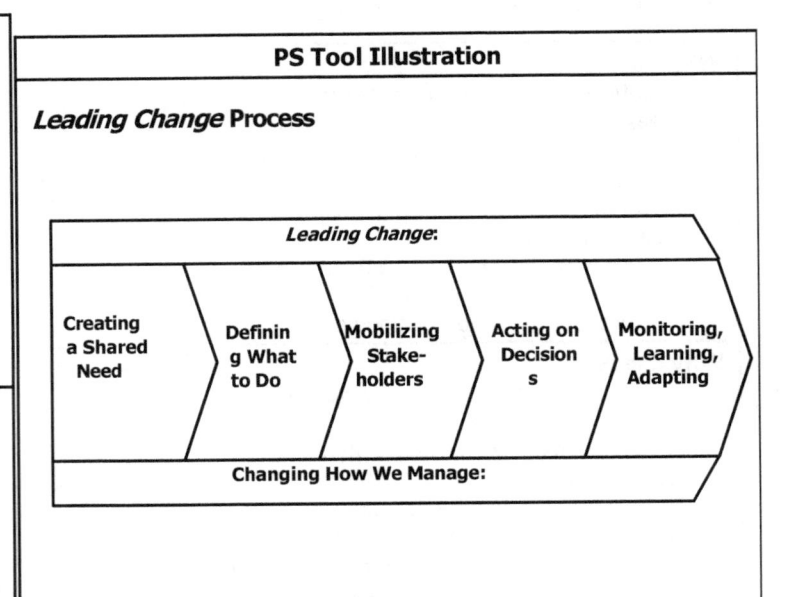

PS Tool Illustration

Leading Change Process

Leading Change:
Creating a Shared Need → Defining What to Do → Mobilizing Stakeholders → Acting on Decisions → Monitoring, Learning, Adapting

Changing How We Manage:

How to use it?
1. Scope the initiative and prepare to implement *Leading Change*
   - Ensure initiative is appropriate for *Leading Change*
   - Educate change leaders and sponsors on *Leading Change*
   - Ensure technical solutions are defined and that an implementation plan developing
2. Set *Leading Change* team up for success
3. Work with trained *Leading Change* coaches and project teams on the following levers:
   - *Leading Change*
   - Creating a shared need
   - Defining what to do
   - Mobilizing stakeholders
   - Acting on decisions
   - Monitoring, learning, and adapting
   - Changing how we manage

Helpful Hints
1. *Leading Change* is an enhancement (but not a replacement) to good project management
2. Trained coaches need to be leveraged to provide support to both leaders and teams
3. *Leading Change* should be implemented under the guidance of a trained professional

PS Tool Summary — Myers-Briggs Type Indicator (MBTI)

What is it?
• A valid and reliable self report instrument that indicates personality type
  – Based on the work of Carl Gustav Jung — one of the founders of modern psychoanalytical theory
  – Based on over 55 years of data
• A framework to understand and communicate differences among team members
	PS Tool Illustration
	MBTI Dimensions:
	
	Where we get our energy
	⟵─────────────⟶
	Extraversion Introversion
	
	How we acquire information
	⟵─────────────⟶
	Sensing Intuition
	
	How decisions are made
	⟵─────────────⟶
	Thinking Feeling
	
	Orientation toward outer world
	⟵─────────────⟶
	Judgment Perception

Why use it?
• To help leaders understand their leadership style and the different styles of their team members
  – Understand how different personalities react to change
• To help individuals understand their personality type and become more successful at relating to others
• To help project teams work more effectively together
  – Gain an appreciation for how we are each predisposed to prefer different things
  – Understand the different ways we communicate and interact with others	

When to use it? • When a new change project team is brought together and they need to gain a quick understanding and appreciation for one another • When project teams are displaying a lack of understanding for one another	

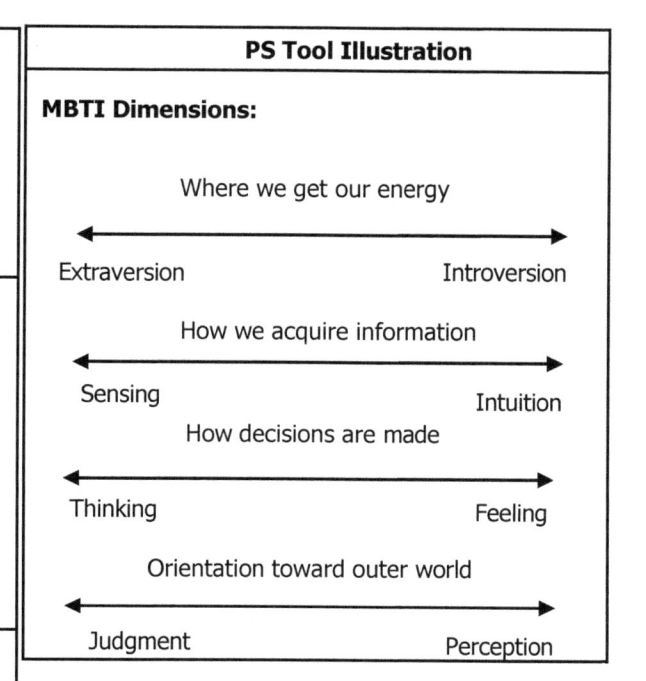

How to use it?
1. A certified MBTI consultant administers the MBTI assessment to individuals
2. The MBTI consultant compiles and summarizes the results of the MBTI assessment
3. The MBTI consultant meets with each individual to discuss their personality type and how it impacts their work
   - How they react to new job situations
   - What makes them comfortable/uncomfortable when interacting with others
4. The MBTI consultant leads a group workshop to discuss how the different personality types can more effectively interact
5. The team identifies 'norms' to govern its working relationships
   - These 'norms' should respect the personality differences identified during the MBTI

Helpful Hints
1. The MBTI should be administered by a trained/certified MBTI resource
2. Participants need to understand that the MBTI is not a test — there are no right or wrong answers
3. Participants should answer the questions with their most natural answer to capture their true personality type
4. There should not be a time limit; Participants should be relaxed when taking the MBTI
5. The MBTI is not designed to measure people, but to sort them into groups

PS Tool Summary — New Leader Transition

What is it?
- A workshop designed to effectively transition a new leader and enable them to lead a highly effective team from the start
- A process for defining how a team will interact under the new leader's direction and for identifying potential issues
    - Note: this tool is not designed to be a problem solving session

Why use it?
- Ensures that a change in leadership does not have a negative impact on an organization's effectiveness
- Allows expectations, concerns, issues, and hopes to be raised as early as possible
    - Sets a climate of openness from the start, where team members speak their mind
- Helps a leader quickly adapt to:
    - An environment of uncertainty, where they are unfamiliar with people, perceptions, and problems
    - Staff unfamiliar with his/her operating style, expectations, or background/capabilities

When to use it?
- Early on (i.e., during the first two weeks) in a new leader's tenure

PS Tool Illustration

Key Questions Addressed During Workshop:

Questions for Leaders	Questions for Staff
• What do I want to know about this group? • What is my job as I currently see it? • What do I want this group to know about me and my leadership style? • What "supervisory" role will I have?	• What do we want to know about this leader? • What are our concerns about this individual becoming our leader? • What do we want most from this leader? • What does this leader need to know about us as a group?
• What are my expectations from this group?	• What is currently in place that we want to keep?

PS Tool Summary — New Leader Transition
(cont'd)

How to use it?
1. The facilitator describes the workshop process to the group
2. The staff work on their set of questions as a group
3. The new leader, in a separate room, responds to a set of questions and writes the responses on a piece of chart paper
• Alternatively, the new leader may respond to the questions in advance, but will leave the room to allow the staff to work on their set of questions as a group
4. The facilitator monitors the process and the time
5. The group and leader reconvene to discuss their responses, asking questions for clarity and understanding
6. The facilitator captures the content on a flip chart
• Agreements reached and actions required are summarized
7. Follow-up sessions are scheduled
• Group session to identify metrics, required process re-design, meeting formats, etc.
• 1:1 meetings between the leader and each staff member to discuss personal visions, challenges, and expectations

Helpful Hints
1. Schedule this session for the first week or two of a new leader's tenure so that the staff and leader have an opportunity to discuss style, expectations, and issues before experiencing them
2. Encourage a meeting between the new leader and old leader
3. Plan on enough time; It is better to over estimate the length of the meeting than to rush it
4. Save discussions about strategic planning and goals for another working session
5. Ensure that follow-up occurs after the meeting

PS Tool Summary — RASIC

What is it?
- RASIC is a tool for analyzing, designing, or re-designing responsibilities and authorities for processes and/or key decisions

Why use it?
- RASIC can help teams:
    1. Identify unclear, overlapping, redundant, "bottle-necked", or inconsistent responsibilities and authorities for processes and/or key decisions
    2. Examine inefficiencies in how an organization structure distributes responsibilities and authorities
    3. Design or re-design clear responsibilities and authorities for processes and key decisions

When to use it?
- RASIC can be applied anytime it is useful to either analyze, design, or re-design responsibilities and authorities
- Although it may be useful to have identified stakeholders prior to applying RASIC, it is not necessary

PS Tool Illustration

Key Decisions/ Process Steps	Individuals/Stakeholders/Roles			
	A	B	C	D
• Decision/Step #1				
• Decision/Step #2				
• Decision/Step #3				

PS Tool Summary — RASIC (cont'd)

How to use it?
1. Clarify the decision or process that is being analyzed, designed, or re-designed
2. Complete the left-hand column of the tool (i.e., Key Decisions or Process Steps)
3. Identify those involved in the decision or process under consideration, and complete the column headings with either position, function, or unit – Usually identifying a position is better than an individual, unless a responsibility lies with a group such as an executive committee, or a product-planning group
4. Complete each cell, identifying those that are responsible (R), have approval authority (A), supports a step (S), is informed (I), or is consulted (C) for each decision or process step
5. Adhere to the following guidelines for: A. Designing/re-designing a process/decision:<ul><li>Only designate one "R" for each decision or step. The "R" should be assigned to a position, not a committee</li><li>Designate an "A" only if necessary; not all steps or decisions may require an "A"</li><li>Ensure that appropriate "S, I, C" are designated, but keep it to necessary involvement only</li></ul> B. Analyzing a current process/decision:<ul><li>If there are multiple "R" or "A" for a step or a decision, note them; Multiple "R" or "A" may be either because there are different views of responsibilities and approvals, or because there actually are multiple "Rs" or "As"</li><li>Be sure to capture all those involved with responsibilities for "S, I, C" since if some of these are not needed in an improved process they will have to be notified of a change</li></ul>

Helpful Hints
1. RASIC is a useful complement to a process map, since it can get into more detailed responsibilities   – Think of a process map at one level of abstraction and RASIC as the next level of detail
2. If a process or key decision is being re-designed/improved, RASIC can help to identify improvements needed
3. In analyzing, designing, or re-designing a process, consider the benefits of pushing responsibilities down — i.e., increasing the level of responsibility from an "S" to an "R," and an "R" to an "A" (if an "A" is needed at all)
4. Be sure to complete a RASIC with those that are either involved in a process or decision, or with those that are very familiar with that process or decision; This tends to reduce the chances of omissions or inaccuracies

PS Tool Summary — Situational Leadership

What is it?
- A tool to help leaders understand the impact of their leadership style on the organization
- A process to help leaders identify when and where to modify their leadership style based on the situation and group/individual readiness
- A series of workshops and coaching to help leaders modify their own leadership style to optimally motivate the group/individual to achieve change goals

Why use it?
- To improve the leader's ability to motivate groups/individuals to adopt a change
- To help leaders understand that different people respond better to different leadership styles, and to adapt their leadership style accordingly
- To improve workforce commitment among groups/individuals based on responding to a leadership style that better fits their readiness level

When to use it?
- During large scale change
- When leaders need to appeal to different degrees of change readiness across the group/individuals
- When leaders are getting excessive pushback from their team members

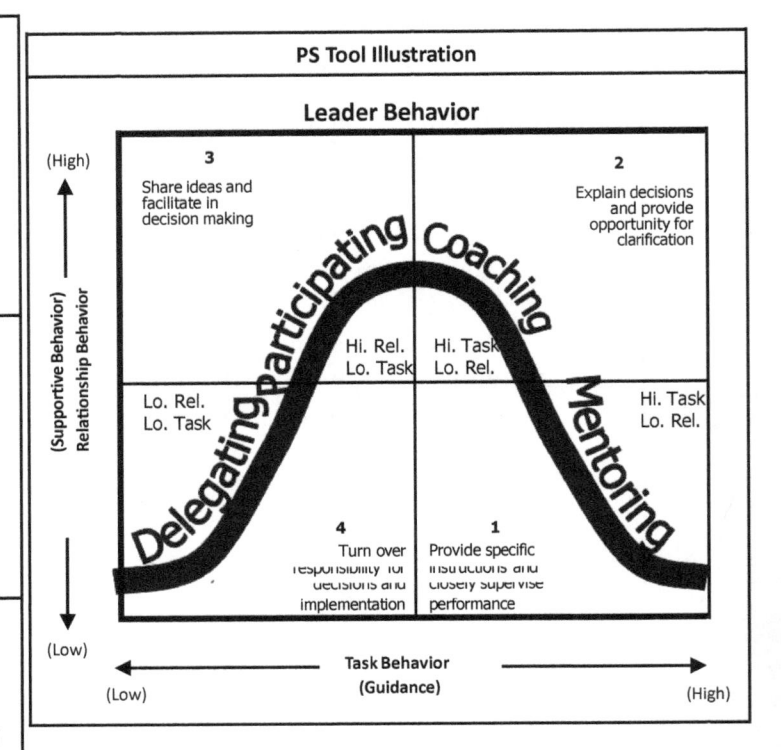

PS Tool Illustration

Leader Behavior

(Supportive Behavior) Relationship Behavior — (Low) to (High)
Task Behavior (Guidance) — (Low) to (High)

Quadrants (Delegating / Participating / Coaching / Mentoring):
- 3: Share ideas and facilitate in decision making — Hi. Rel. Lo. Task (Participating)
- 2: Explain decisions and provide opportunity for clarification — Hi. Task Hi. Rel. (Coaching)
- 4: Turn over responsibility for decisions and implementation — Lo. Rel. Lo. Task (Delegating)
- 1: Provide specific instructions and closely supervise performance — Hi. Task Lo. Rel. (Mentoring)

How to use it?

Through workshops and individual one-on-one coaching:
1. Coach leaders to identify their primary leadership style
    - Leadership styles vary according to task behavior and relationship behavior
    - A range of behaviors are associated with each leadership style
    - A leadership style will have different impacts depending on the group/individual and situation
2. Identify the needs and change readiness of groups/individuals regarding a particular situation
    - The needs of the change initiative need to be clearly defined
    - Readiness is defined as the willingness, confidence, and ability of a group/individual to do a task
3. Help leaders develop skills to alter their leadership style to fit different situations
    - Demonstrate the appropriate leadership style for handling different situations
    - Show how to change one's leadership style according to a specific business or relationship situation
    - Demonstrate how to use different types of behavior to build employees' readiness to fulfill increasingly challenging tasks
    - Practice implementation of Situational Leadership tools and techniques

PS Tool Summary — Situational Leadership (cont'd)

Helpful Hints
1. It is imperative for leaders to understand the needs of the group/individual to effectively modify ones leadership style
2. There is no 'one-size-fits-all' leadership style; Each leadership style can be modified to effectively meet the needs of a group/individual
3. Leverage results of a Myers-Briggs assessment to better understand individuals on a team

PS Tool Summary — Stakeholder Analysis

What is it? • To provide a framework to assess the needed and likely support required by key stakeholders for the successful implementation of the team's changes

Why use it?
• To help analyze key stakeholders:
  1. Identify the likely position regarding the team's solution (i.e., negative, neutral, positive)
  2. Determine the degree of support needed from a key stakeholder to have at least a reasonable probability for a successful implementation of the changes
  3. Analyze the most critical gaps between where stakeholder support is needed and where it exists, and plan for closing the gaps

When to use it? • When it is necessary to mobilize stakeholders • Following the application of scoping tools (i.e., Is/Is Not, In the Frame/Out of the Frame; SIPOC + Start/Stop), vision tools (i.e., Backward Imaging, Visioning Questions), and tools for making the vision actionable (i.e., More of/Less of, Bulls-Eye Chart)

Note: (1) Individuals, teams, units, positions

	PS Tool Illustration				
	Stakeholders' Position on the Initiative				
Key Stakeholders[1]	- -	-	+	+ +	**Reasons for Current Position; Actions Required to Alter Position**

PS Tool Summary — Stakeholder Analysis (cont'd)

How to use it?

1. List the key stakeholders in approximate descending order of impact on the successful implementation of the team's changes
   – This step can be done ahead of time if a Key Constituents Map has been previously completed
2. For each stakeholder, determine their likely position regarding the proposed changes; i.e., whether they are likely to be very positive (++), positive (+), neutral (0), negative (-), or very negative (--)
   – Draw an X to note their current position
3. For each stakeholder, identify the degree of support needed to enable successful implementation of desired changes — draw an O to note the needed position — and draw an arrow connecting the X and O for each stakeholder
4. Discuss and note the key actions that are likely to be required to shift key stakeholders' positions. These actions should be integrated into the team's Action Plan

Helpful Hints
1. Encourage the team not to get too distracted by the incremental ratings — they are meant only as a rough approximation of a position; i.e., whether a key stakeholder is negative or very negative is less important than where they need to be and how the team plans on moving them there 2. Determine which stakeholders are likely to influence the position of other stakeholders (this may already be done if they are listed in order of impact, but not necessarily)   – For example, if a business unit's executive committee is a key stakeholder, their position may sway other stakeholders that are subordinate in the organizational hierarchy — not by asserting hierarchical control, but by helping persuade reluctant stakeholders 3. Based on the above tip, determine if there is a logical order/sequence to any actions that are identified for shifting key stakeholders' positions

PS Tool Summary — Stakeholder Workshop

What is it?
- A workshop designed to teach leaders how to engage stakeholders
- A tool to help teams determine required interventions to increase stakeholder buy-in, ownership, and engagement

Why use it?
- To better understand how to build stakeholder engagement
- To "baseline" a team's progress re: stakeholder buy-in (strengths and progress)
- To identify key activities required to increase the level of engagement of key stakeholders

When to use it?
- During the planning stages for any large scale change
- When stakeholders do not appear to be as engaged as they should be
- When stakeholder buy-in, ownership, and engagement is critical for success

PS Tool Illustration

Stakeholder Plot:

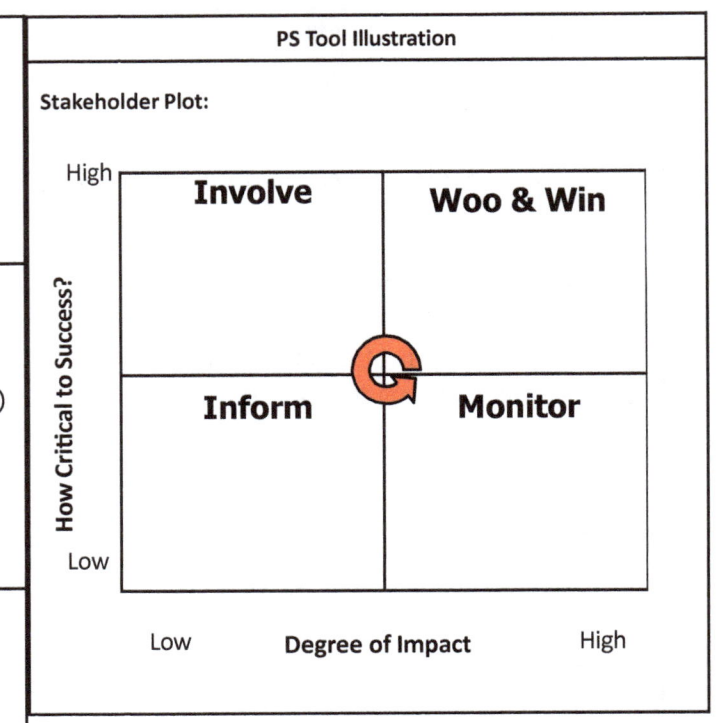

	Low Degree of Impact	High Degree of Impact
High How Critical to Success?	Involve	Woo & Win
Low How Critical to Success?	Inform	Monitor

PS Tool Summary — Stakeholder Workshop (cont'd)

How to use it?

Stakeholder Engagement Workshop Steps:
1. Identify key stakeholders
2. Identify signs of stakeholder ownership/buy-in
   - On-going leadership commitment
   - Shared need/understanding among impacted individuals
   - Mobilized
3. Assess stakeholder buy-in
4. Schedule a workshop to discuss proven methods/approaches for building and sustaining stakeholder buy-in and engagement
   - Identifying key stakeholders
   - Predicting resistance and support
   - Engaging people in the project
   - Minimizing/resolving resistance to change
5. Clarify roles/responsibilities for Program/Project Managers, Leadership Teams, and Global Program Office Leaders, and Operating leadership
6. Review techniques for dealing with stakeholders

Helpful Hints
1. Stakeholders are defined as people, internal or external to the organization, involved in and/or impacted by a change   - Key stakeholders have power, influence, or authority over the project 2. Stakeholders should be involved in all phases of the project — not just deployment 3. The workshop should include several breakouts so project teams can actually create stakeholder plans 4. Leverage the ChangeFast assessment as an exercise during the working

PS Tool Summary — Strategic Visioning (Grove)

What is it?
- A process and set of visuals tools designed to combine the best practices of strategic planning, visioning, and large scale change

Why use it?
- Facilitates big-picture thinking, participation, and ownership from everyone involved in the strategic visioning process
- Enables leaders to guide their teams to develop a compelling vision of the future and the strategies needed to make it a reality
    - Achieve consensus on important factors by creating a venue where everyone contributes and is heard
    - Tap group creativity by using processes that stimulate the organization
    - Create visual maps of organizational processes that become a group memory

When to use it?
- When defining the vision of a large scale change (or other initiative)

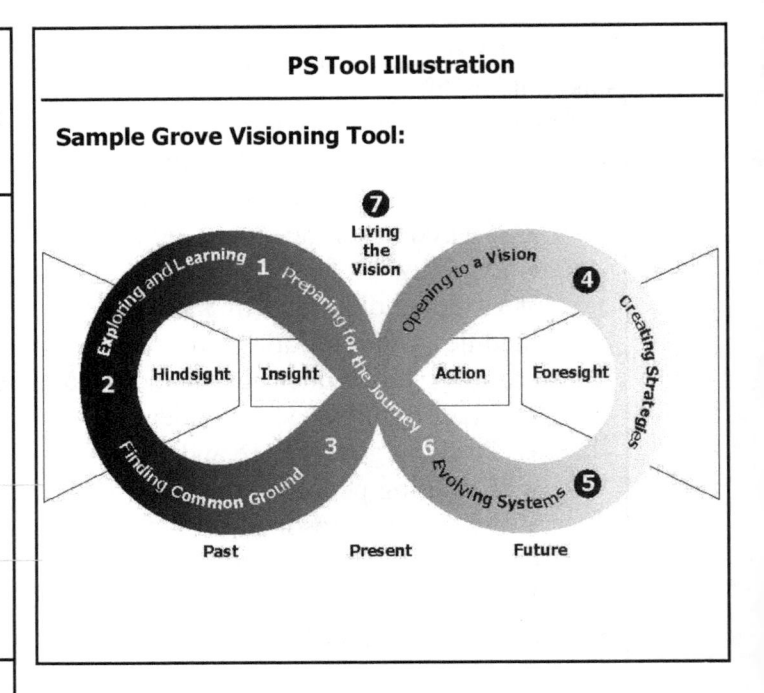

PS Tool Illustration

Sample Grove Visioning Tool:

Stages around the infinity loop:
1. Preparing for the Journey (Exploring and Learning)
2. Hindsight
3. Finding Common Ground
4. Opening to a Vision / Creating Strategies
5. Evolving Systems
6. (Foresight / Action)
7. Living the Vision

Center boxes: Hindsight | Insight | Action | Foresight

Timeline: Past — Present — Future

How to use it?
1. Prepare for the strategic visioning process
• Clearly define the large scale change
• Identify key stakeholders (champions, leaders, project team, etc.)
2. Review and understand the organization's history and environment
• Plot key events on the history plot
3. Agree upon the driving need for the large scale change
• Identify any boundaries that need to be respected
4. Develop a vision of the future state
• Brainstorm future states that will resolve the key issues driving the large scale change
5. Create strategies to achieve the PS vision
• Identify the activities required to turn the vision into action
• Develop implementation plan to achieve the vision
6. Engage stakeholders in the PS vision
• Develop a plan to inform and involve all stakeholders in achieving the vision
7. Implement action plan to achieve future state
• Demonstrate leadership and commitment during the implementation

PS Tool Summary — Strategic Visioning (Grove) (cont'd)

Helpful Hints
1. While the business leader champions the strategic visioning process, the entire team needs to be involved
2. Results of the strategic visioning process should be reviewed periodically during the change implementation

PS Tool Summary — Task Oriented Team Development (TOTD)

What is it?	PS Tool Illustration
<ul><li>A model to build a high-performing team by improving its ability to manage interdependencies and get jobs done effectively</li><li>A questionnaire and series of workshops to help teams identify/develop their:<ul><li>Goals and Objectives</li><li>Roles and Responsibilities</li><li>Procedures</li><li>Interpersonal Relationships</li></ul></li></ul>	**TOTD Hierarchy of Team Needs** (Pyramid from top to bottom:) - Interpersonal Relationships - Systems/Procedures - Roles - Goals

Why use it?
- To avoid poor teamwork stemming from poorly defined/conflicting goals, roles, or procedures
  - Interpersonal team conflicts are often a symptom of inappropriate goals, roles, or procedures
  - Interpersonal relationships tend to suffer as a result of the other team dynamics
- To help a team achieve:
  - A high degree of confidence/ trust in each other
  - Respect for each others' opinions
  - Highly motivated participants
  - A supportive and open environment for problem solving and decision making activities

When to use it?
- When a new change project team is brought together and they need to gain a quick understanding and appreciation for one another
- When a team exhibits a need for development

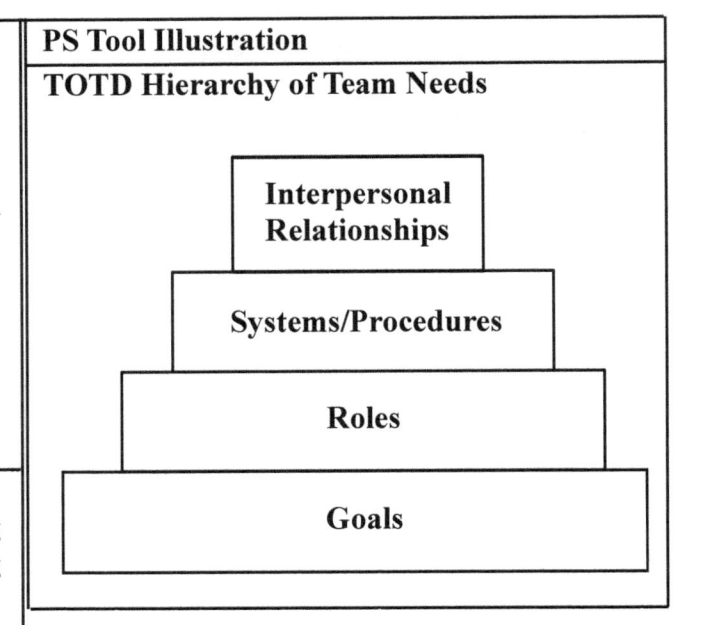

PS Tool Summary — TOTD (cont'd)

How to use it?

1. Identify whether team development is required
   • Consider team development whenever interdependencies exist
   • Introduce team development when there is a need to set goals, make plans, enhance communication, reduce redundant activities, or enhance problem-solving
2. Define the **purpose** of the team
   • Ensure the team's mission and objectives are understood and accepted by all team members
3. Define the **roles** of each team member
   • Identify what each team member expects of each other
   • Introduce techniques for dealing with conflict
4. Define the **systems** that support the team
   • Identify the support systems that are needed/already in place
   • Determine whether the systems promote teamwork
5. Define the **relationships** within the team
   • Identify the extent to which people trust, support, respect, and feel about each other
   • Further develop interpersonal team relationships

Helpful Hints
1. While the TOTD materials can be self-administered, a facilitator/consultant who is not part of the work group can help to identify hidden issues 2. A team requires development if it expends excessive energy on activities outside of the task at hand 3. Team development should be scheduled, similar to a *planned maintenance* checkup for a car, designed to prevent major breakdowns in team functioning

PS Tool Summary — Vroom Decision Making Model

What is it?
• Decision making model that guides leaders to select either a participative or autocratic decision process depending on the situation surrounding the decision

Why use it?
• To guide a leader to select the most effective decision making process, based on the situation and the expected outcomes   – Decision making model selected to ensure short-term results and minimize risk of failure • Considers key factors such as degree of team acceptance and potential conflict that may arise from the decision • To help leaders understand the attributes of both good and bad decisions

When to use it?
• When a key decision is required as part of a change process

PS Tool Illustration
Decision Making Alternatives: <u>Autocratic</u> A1 — Leader makes the decision based on information available at the time A2 — Leader makes the decision, based on information obtained from team <u>Collaborative</u> C1 — Leader shares the decision with individual team members to obtain their ideas/suggestions, and then makes the decision C2 — Leader shares the decision with the group collectively to obtain their ideas/suggestions, and then makes the decision <u>Group</u> Leader shares the decision with the group and reaches consensus on the solution with the group

PS Tool Summary — Vroom Decision Making Model (cont'd)

How to use it?

1. Leader evaluates the decision according to:
   - Decision Quality — extent to which decisions made will impact team performance
   - Decision Acceptance — extent to which outcome dependent on the team's acceptance
   - Timeliness — time available to make decisions
2. Leader assesses the advantages of using a participative or autocratic decision making process

Participative Process Advantages	Autocratic Process Advantages
- Accesses a greater pool of knowledge - Provides different perspectives - Ensures greater comprehension - Increases acceptance - Demonstrates that Leader has a high degree of trust for team - Allows for brainstorming when solution is not straight-forward	- Avoids "groupthink," minority domination or social pressures - Minimizes subjectivity when the group faces environmental threats or potential serious impacts from the decision - Enables a quick turnaround on the decision - Is based on clear/well-structured facts

3. Leader selects from one of three decision processes:
   - Autocratic — Leader makes the decision
   - Consultative — Leader obtains input from team and then makes the decision
   - Group — Leader engages the team to discuss and make the decision

Helpful Hints

1. Rely on your intuition/understanding of the group when selective a decision making process
2. Consider the resulting commitment and potential conflict that may arise as a result of the decision making process selected
3. Lean towards decision making processes that offer short-term results and minimize the risk of failure

PS Tool Summary — William Bridges Change and Transition Model

What is it?
- A model to help leaders understand the social/people aspects of a change
- A process to help lead employees through the transition associated with a large scale change
  - Change refers to a situation (e.g., new boss, new policy) and is external
  - Transition refers to the psychological process people go through to come to terms with the new situation

Why use it?
- Ensures that the transition is handled appropriately
  - Transition occurs with every change
  - If the transition is not handled appropriately, the change will not be successful
- Helps leaders understand the three stages of transition and how they can move their team through each of the three stages
- Helps project teams understand what they are going through
- Helps leaders understand that transition is not automatic
- To set expectations for the social factors impacting a change

When to use it?
- During large scale change to help teams understand the ending and beginning stages

PS Tool Illustration

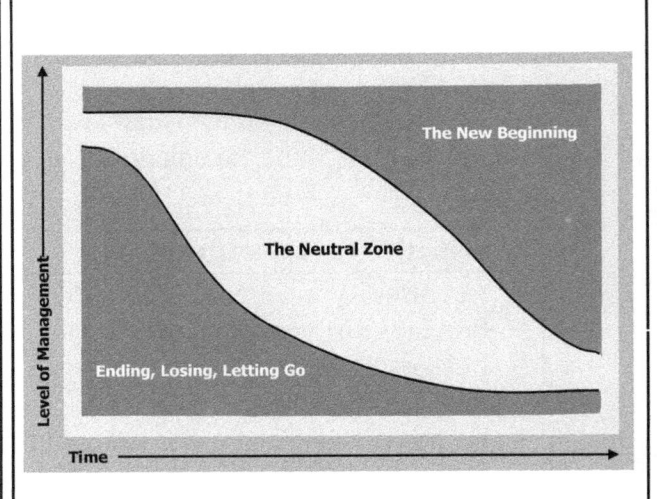

The three transition stages: Ending/Saying Goodbye to old processes, The Neutral Zone, and The new beginning (new process)

Note: Material is copyrighted; Permission required to use tool

PS Tool Summary — William Bridges
Change and Transition Model (cont'd)

How to use it?

1. Describe the change and why it must happen
    • Leaders need to be able to do so succinctly
2. Carefully plan the details of the change
    • Assign responsibility for each detail
    • Establish timelines
    • Develop a communications plan
3. Identify who is going to have to let go of what
    • Define what is ending and what is not
    • Define the things that people should let go of
4. Help people to respectfully let go of the past
    • Establish events that symbolize that the change has come
    • Demonstrate understanding for 'grieving'
5. Communicate with people through the neutral zone with the following messages:
    • Purpose: Why the change is occurring
    • Picture: What it will look and feel like once we reach our goal
    • Plan: Step-by-step guide to reaching our goal
    • Part: What each employee can do to help achieve the goal
6. Create temporary solutions to temporary problems
7. Help people launch the new beginning
    • Articulate the new attitudes/behaviors needed to make the change work
    • Provide opportunities to exhibit and reward these attitudes/behaviors

Helpful Hints
1. Ensure that leaders understand the difference between 'change' and 'transition' 2. Since 'transitions' are a significant part of 'changes,' timelines should keep the necessary transitions in mind 3. The higher up a person is in the organization, the less time they tend to take to move through the change process 4. It would be beneficial to have an experienced facilitator lead the use of this tool

Appendix
- **Tool Templates and Background**

7-S Model: Worksheet

> **Instructions**
> 1. Clearly define the change process/strategy
> 2. Identify key issues that may arise due to the change for:
>   - Shared values
>   - Strategy
>   - Structure
>   - Staff
>   - Skills
>   - Systems
>   - Style

Organizational Elements	Key Issues to Address	Timing	Key Owner
Shared Vision			
Strategy			
Structure			
Staff			
Skills			
Systems			
Style			

Beckhard's Model: Worksheet

Instructions:

1. Define the present state
2. Clearly outline the desired state and communicate this to the key stakeholders
3. Identify the characteristics that can be expected during the transition state
4. Develop action plans to help move an organization through the transition state

Social Issues
- How will the group relate to one another?
- How will relationships be impacted?
- How will interpersonal group relationships change?

Political Issues
- How can we make this situation win-win?
- What hidden agendas exist?
- Who needs to be engaged/advised? Who are the key stakeholders?

Technical Issues
- What are the process/technical/system changes required to get to the desired state?

Present State:	Key Issues to Address During Transition State:
Desired State:	

The clearer both the present and desired states, the easier the transition is to manage

Note: While an experience PS resource would be helpful, project teams could implement this tool without assistance

Bulls-Eye Chart: Worksheet

Instructions:

1. Identify the mission/vision for the initiative
2. Discuss the required changes in attitudes/perceptions necessary to support the change
3. Identify specific actions/behaviors that will create/reinforce the mindset and achieve the mission

Making A Vision Actionable

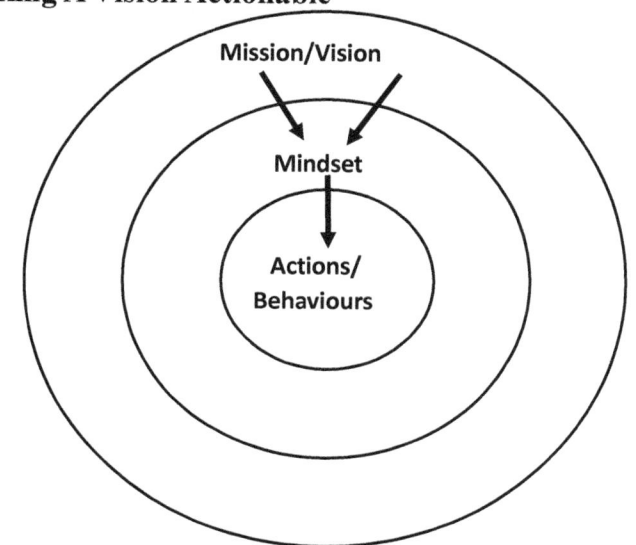

(Bullseye diagram: outer ring "Mission/Vision", middle ring "Mindset", center "Actions/Behaviours")

A. Mission/Vision

B. Desired Actions/Behavioral Changes

(More of)
1.
2.
3.
4.
5.
etc.

(Less of)
1.
2.
3.
4.
5.
etc.

Stating the vision in actionable, behavioral terms helps the team gain commitment and identify sources of resistance

Cog's Ladder: Worksheet

Instructions: 1. Schedule a team workshop 2. Introduce the team to Cog's ladder: the different stages of team development 3. Determine what stage the group is currently in 4. Identify next steps to moving up the ladder		**What stage do we appear to be stuck?**

Phases of Group Development	Characteristics	Why are we stuck at this stage?
Esprit	• Intense group loyalty, unspoken communication, high trust level, extremely high task accomplishment	
Constructive	• Flexible thinking, strong communication, open information, collaboration, focus on accomplishing the task	**What do we need to do to move up the ladder?**
Bid for Power	• Conflict, cliques, emerging leaders	
Why We're Here	• Clarification of tasks, goals, and roles	
Polite	• Getting acquainted, low task accomplishment	

Note: Use of the Cog's ladder tool would benefit greatly from an experienced facilitator

Denison Culture Audit: Worksheet

Instructions:

1. Review the Denison Culture Audit and add open ended questions as appropriate
2. Have a certified consultant administer the audit (questionnaire) to employees
3. Identify key cultural issues that need to be addressed based on audit results
4. Design action plans to address these cultural issues

Audit Results — Illustration

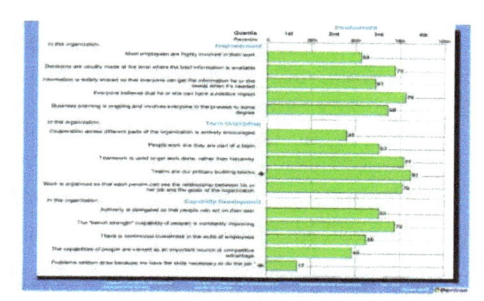

Action Plan Based on Survey Results

Cultural Traits	Linkage to Business Results	Issues to Address	Action Plan
• Involvement	• ROI, Quality, Employee Satisfaction, Product Development		
• Consistency	• ROI, ROA, ROS, Quality, Employee Satisfaction		
• Adaptability	• Revenue, Sales Growth, Market Share, Product Growth, Innovation		
• Mission	• Revenue, Sales Growth, Market Share, ROI, ROA, ROS		

Note: The Denison Culture Audit needs to be administered by a certified consultant

The Elevator Speech: Worksheet

Instructions:

1. Imagine a chance meeting with a key stakeholder in an elevator
2. The key stakeholder asks, "I heard you are working on the _____ initiative. What's it all about?"
3. Prepare & practice a short answer to that question that can be delivered in 30 seconds or less

Guidelines: Good Elevator Speeches normally contain:
- Here's what our initiative is about
- Here's why it is important
- Here's what we need to change
- Here's what success will look like
- Here's what we need from you

My Elevator Speech:

GDQ: Worksheet

Instructions:

1. Administer GDQ questionnaire to group
2. Compile and summarize GDQ results
3. Review results as a group
   - Discuss strengths and weaknesses
4. Develop action plan to address group development needs

Group Strengths	Group Development Needs	Next Steps/Action Plan

Note: The GDQ needs to be administered by a certified consultant

MBTI: Worksheet

Instructions:

1. A certified MBTI consultant administers the MBTI
2. During a workshop or one-on-one coaching, the MBTI consultant helps individuals understand how their personality type impacts their work and working relationships
3. The MBTI consultant leads a group workshop to discuss how the different personality types can more effectively interact
4. The team identifies 'norms' to govern its working relationships

My Personality Style:

Circle Appropriate Dimension

Extroversion	Introversion
Sensing	Intuition
Thinking	Feeling
Judgment	Perception

How My Personality Type Is Demonstrated in My Work

-
-
-

Things I Should Consider When Interacting With Others

-
-
-

Note: The MBTI needs to be administered by a certified MBT consultant

New Leader Transition: Worksheet

Instructions:
1. The staff work on their set of questions as a group
2. The new leader responds to a set of questions in a separate room
3. The group and leader reconvene to discuss their responses, asking questions for clarity and understanding

Team Background Template

Background Highlights Personal: Professional:	**A major challenge the new leader will face in this role:**
What I bring to this group and what makes it a contribution:	**What it is like to work here (and why):**

RASIC: Worksheet

Instructions:
1. Identify/list key decisions or process steps
2. Identify/list all individuals/groups involved
3. Complete the matrix by assigning R/A/S/I/C as appropriate

Guidelines:
- Only one "R" allowed per decision/step
- Multiple "A's" are discouraged — a "S" might be more appropriate
- "R/A" is the only combination allowed

R — Responsible (Takes lead on)(1)
A — Approve (Final decision)
S — Supports (Actively assists)
I — Informed (Made aware)
C — Consulted (Provides advice)

Key Decisions or Process Steps	Individuals/Stakeholders/Roles						
• Decision/Step #1 • Decision/Step #2 • Decision/Step #3							

Note: (1) Only one "R" per decision

Situational Leadership: Worksheet

Instructions:
1. During the workshop and one-on-one coaching sessions:
2. Identify the leader's primary leadership style
3. Identify the needs of the group/individuals
4. Help the leader to modify his/her leadership style to correspond to the group/individual's needs and maximize performance

Leadership Styles

Task Behavior	Relationship Behavior
• Extent to which the leader engages in defining roles telling what, how, when, where, and who is to do what	• Extent to which the leader engages in two-way communication, listening, facilitating, and supporting

▼

Leader's Primary Leadership Style:

Group/Individual Characteristics

Characteristics	Level Displayed (Circle level)
• Ability (group/individual has the necessary knowledge, experience, and skill)	H M L
• Willingness (group/individual has the necessary confidence, commitment, and motivation)	H M L
• Confident (group/individual has the necessary assurance and conviction)	H M L

A different leadership style should be used depending on the group/individual's level of readiness

Stakeholder Analysis: Worksheet

Instructions:

1. Identify all stakeholders as specifically as possible
2. Identify your perception of their current position regarding the initiative
3. Draw an arrow to where each stakeholder needs to be in order to succeed
4. Identify actions required to influence critical stakeholders

Key Stakeholders(1)	Stakeholders' Position on the Initiative				Reasons for Current Position; Actions Required to Alter Position
	- -	-	+	++	
Etc.					

Note: (1) Individuals, teams, units, positions

Strategic Visioning (Grove): Worksheet

Instructions:

1. Review and understand the organization's history and environment
2. Agree upon the driving need for the change
3. Develop a vision of the future state
4. Create strategies to achieve the PS vision
5. Engage stakeholders in the PS vision
6. Implement action plan to achieve future state

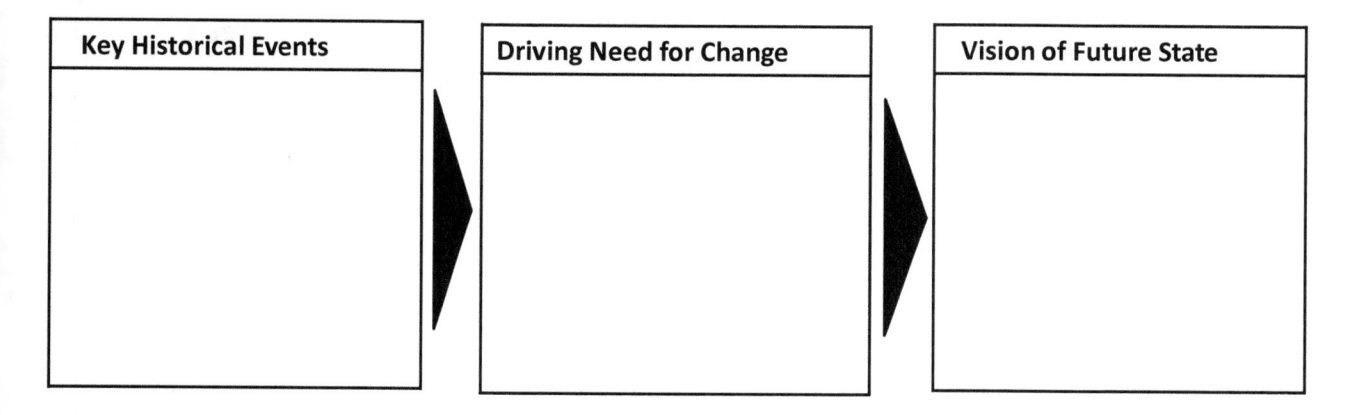

Key Historical Events	Driving Need for Change	Vision of Future State

The team needs to define a detailed action plan to achieve the vision, making sure to engage key stakeholders

Task Oriented Team Development (TOTD): Worksheet

Instructions:	Team Goals/Objectives
1. Define the **goals/objectives** of the team 2. Define the **roles/responsibilities** of each team member 3. Define the **key processes** that support the team 4. Determine whether interpersonal team relationships are suffering as a result of goals/objectives, roles/responsibilities, or key processes 5. Develop action plan, addressing areas of conflict	*Obtain consensus within group*

Key Roles/ Responsibilities	Team Member
1.	
2.	
3.	
4.	
5.	

Key Processes	Steps
A)	1. 2. 3.
B)	1. 2. 3.
C)	1. 2. 3.

Interpersonal relationship conflicts tend to suffer from conflicts surrounding goals, roles, or processes

Vroom Decision Making Process: Worksheet

Instructions:
1. Evaluate the decision according to key criteria
2. Assess the advantages of both participative and autocratic decision making processes
3. Select appropriate decision making process

Timelines	Ranking (Circle One)
• Does the decision timeline allow for group input?	H M L

Criteria Used to Evaluate Decision

Decision Quality	Ranking (Circle One)
• How important is the technical quality of the decision?	H M L
• To what extent do group members have sufficient information to make a high quality decision?	H M L
• To what extent does the lead have sufficient information to make a high- quality decision?	H M L
• How well structured is the decision?	H M L

Decision Acceptance	Ranking (Circle One)
• How important is group commitment?	H M L
• Does the leader have sufficient information to make a high-quality decision?	H M L
• If the leader made the decision alone, would the group be committed?	H M L
• Will conflict likely occur from the decision?	H M L
• Do group members share the organizational goals to be obtained in solving the problem?	H M L

The Vroom Decision Making Process workshop helps leaders to select the optimal decision making process based on the above information

William Bridges Change and Transition Model: Worksheet

Instructions for Leaders:	Brief Compelling Reason Why Change Must Happen:
1. Describe the change and why it must happen 2. Identify who is going to have to let go of what 3. Identify key messages for employees impacted by the change 4. Communicate with people through the neutral zone with the following messages: 5. Create temporary solutions to temporary problems 6. Help people launch the new beginning	

Key Messages for Employees Impacted by Change

Purpose (Why we have to do this)	**Picture** (What it will look and feel like when we reach our goal)	**Plan** (How we will get there)	**Part** (What you can/need to do to help us get there)

Sources

Bridges, W. & Bridges, S. (2019) *Transitions*. Da Capo Lifelong Books.

Brown, K. (2017). *The Cambridge Handbook of Workplace Training and Employee Development*. Cambridge University Press.

Flores, B, (2023) *ATD's Organization Development Handbook.* Association for Talent Development.

Foster, G., Grannell, C. (2022) *Essential Management Models: Tried and Tested Business Frameworks for Strategy, Customers and Growth*. Routledge.

Ross, S. (2019). *Training and Development in Organization: An essential Guide For Trainers*, Routledge.

Silverman, M. (2002). *The Consultant's Big Book of Organization Development Tools: 50 Reproducible Intervention Tools to Help Solve Your Clients' Problem*. McGraw.

Printed in the USA
CPSIA information can be obtained
at www.ICGtesting.com
CBHW081931051224
18487CB00050B/928